T0368496

The painter
of the camps
# of death

ALBUM

LEK PERVIZI

The Painter ofe the camps of death

**Drawings by the Authour
prisoner in the deportation camps**

*To all the victims
who suffered
in prisons
and in the camps of death
of the communist dictatorship,
to small children
symbols of innocence
who lost their lives
in the infamous camp
by Tepelenë
holocaust
to the bloody idol
of communism.*

Pr.Dr. Agron Tufa

Director of the Institute of Studies
of Crimes of Communism, (ISKK) Tirana.

Foreword

The album of this edition of the Institute for the Study of Communist Crimes (ISKK) presents to us a reality of a little known Albania, perhaps just ignored, of little that has survived the communist hell. A representative selection of these paintings that we present on this album, survived the hell of the dictatorship, fortunately, with their author, "the painter of the loa dead camps", as they are called. Lek Pervizi, painter, writer, poet, publicist, historian and translator, he is a memorial of the living archive with boundless energy, even though he is 90 years old. Lek Pervizi is probably the most precise realization of an inflexible character. Author of these paintings, portraits, graphics and drawings he is alive in the majority of drawings, characters out of his pen. They come to us as an echo of a tragic past of inhumanity thanks to circumstantial tools, pencils, or charcoal, he used. The portraits of intellectuals were constantly put in pieces of circumstantial paper, by the young painter, who shared with them the same suffering of this frightening Calvary. he courage to remain spiritually strong not to yield in these terror camps, to the police, or to the crushing of forced labor, to hunger and great suffering. Each portrait and drawing in these creations of the painter transmits something. Emerging from the abyss of communist hell circles, they seem to crack the night of barbarian times in the middle of the 20th century. So in the mists of the time slot by drawings, we see the parade of personalities of science, art, thought and Albanian nobility: Prof. Ali Cungu, Dr. Mitat Araniti, Dr. Nedim Kokona, his brother Valentine Pervizi, Dr. Ibrahim Sokoli, Prof. Guljem Deda, Dr. Sander Saraci, Dr. Loro Muzhani, Dr. Ali Erebara, Prof. Dr. Lazer Radi, Dr. Latif Spahiu, Dr. Estref Frasheri, Prince Ded Gjomarkaj, students: Victor Dosti, Ylber Starova, Thabit Rusi, Tomorri

Dine, Reshit Mulleti, Ernest Dosti. Montagnards: Pjeter Bardheci, Llesh Doda, Gjin Lleshi, Nikoll Paluca, Bajazit Kaloshi, the author's granddaughters, Eva and Edi, his mother, and portraits of his wife Beba, the painter's sons, Leonard, Dorian, Aurel. Paintings, drawings, and scenes, studies by Lek Pervizi, were not created under normal conditions, to present them in the eyes of the assessment of juries in any part, exhibition, or jubilee of liberation. He had taken the courage to demonstrate the existence of the horrors of this death camp, under the cruelty of a club and the torture of police officers, as presented to us in the scenes drawn inside the camp and forced labor. These dark scenes, drawings and compositions, the generation of today fails to conceive. Now, at the moment when we, with dignity, should largely approach the Albanian "Auschwitz", like Vloçishtit, Beden, Tepelenë, Porto Palermo, to our unspeakable shame, we do not find stone on stone! Neither prisons, nor forced labor and concentration or extermination camps. It seems that the testimonies of those who confess these atrocities took place once before, in prehistoric times. Because the topography of the pain of these inhuman tiredness did not leave a single sign. . Ouch! It was not like other former communist countries, where prisons and extermination camps were returned to human memory. The old prisons and internment camps in Albania have almost disappeared from the earth under the greed of industrial and agricultural projects. The only clue to testify are the drawings, portraits and studies of Lek Pervizi, recognized as: the Painter of the death camps.

Deportation camp of Tepelenë 1948-1954

Ruins of the Tepelenë deportation camp, what remains to this day.

After the Tepelenë camp, it was Savër de Lushnjë's camp, the most important, where Tepelene's internees were transferred and housed in these barracks, 1954-1990.

TEPELENE DEPORTATION CAMP
Drawing of a flight of birds from the original by the painter Lek Pervizi deported to this camp, 1950-1954.

It is thanks to Lek Pervizi, that we were able to know the real image of the deportation camp of Tepelenë, in the absence of non-existent photos, that the ruined walls of the barracks. With these drawings, the author deeply shocked Albanian and foreign public opinion.

General view of a barracks, which shows how they were locked up and piled up the deportees, whole families, old people, women and children.

View of the construction of barracks with wooden scaffolding used as litter, built by the Italian army. The communist dictatorship changed these barracks to the detention of thousands of innocent Albanians.

Drawing showing the situation of the deportees on two-storey wooden scaffolding used as primitive housing, below the families, old, women and children, above the men, who were subjected to forced labor

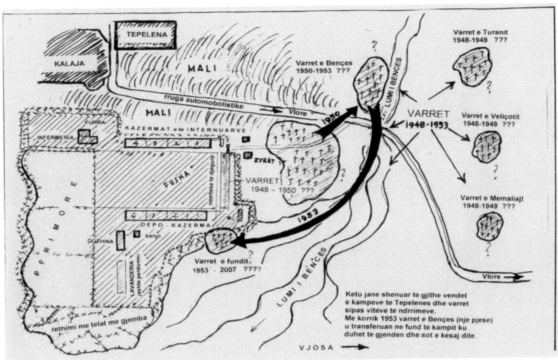

Map showing where the Tepelenë camp was located, with the barracks.
The camp was surrounded by barbed wire hedges to prevent any escape. We show where the graves of the internees were scattered. In addition, these graves had been transferred three times. The cemetery which had formed in front of the camp was plowed with a tractor and sown with oats.

Women and girls were treated like cargo animals, carrying heavy weights of wood, by dozens of kilometers of steep paths, from dawn to evening, under the care of criminal-minded armed police.

Men were subjected to forced labor, carrying large tree trunks on their shoulders,
pilots for mines and other heavy objects, threatened by police rifles.

Women suffering under the heavy weight of the load of wood

10

The 15-year-old girls were subjected to heavy labor as pack animals.
They grew and aged in the deportation camps like true heroines, proud and proud, indomitable.

The massacre of children in the Tepelenë camp. In a single night in August 1948 33 children died
at an early age, by an angry epidemic, followed by the daily deaths of other children and the elderly

Tepelene

The painter's mother, first drawing, 1951

Brother Valentin, second drawing, 1951

In these small sketches we show how Valentin, from his arrival in Albania, is arrested and put in prison and the deportation camps of the dictatorship, 47 years old, 1944-1991. The verses down tell her story.

You threw me into proud fights against the Germans,

You helped me escape from the germen camp

You saved me from aerial bombardment

In Vienna you carried me and denied the stay

In a perilous journey you sent me

Arrived in Albania, locked me in priso

After you deported me to the city of Berat

You made fun of me transferring to Tirana

You unjustly lock me in a fortress;

16

Finally you, very cruel, subjected me to forced labor.

As a beast of burden in the Tepelenë camp
Destiny, destiny why you treated me like this
leave me at the mercy of evil?

Fate, fate how did you motivate yourself so unfair?

Valentin had to endure 47 years of prisons and deportation camp, and worse, 47 years separated from his wife, forced to rempatrier in Italy. The couple finally, surpassed the Myth of Ulysses and Penelope, could kiss after 47 years of separation and suffering.

17

Brother Valentin, Tepelenë,1951, 47 years prisonier.

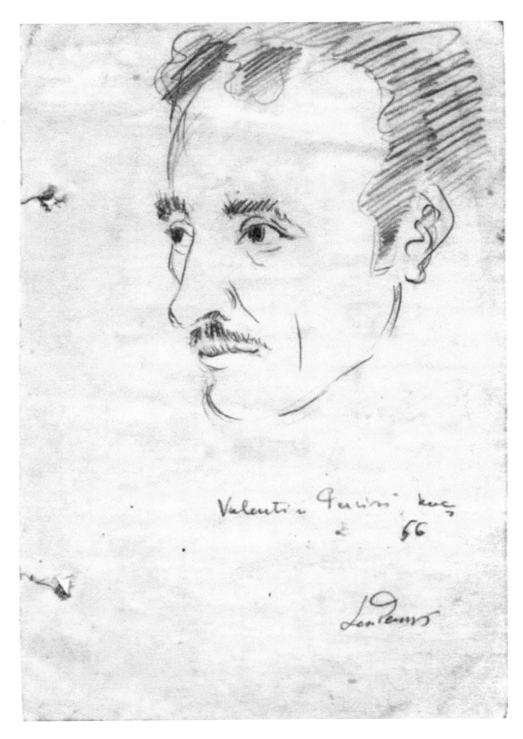

Le frère ainé Valentin Pervizi (47)

Llesh Doda of Mirdita (7)

Her son, Gjin Lleshi (16)

Melson
Tepelene 51

Montagnard de Vermosh (7)

Paysan of Myzeqeya (7)

The Tepelenë fortress drawn from a barracks window.

**Drawing of 650 gr. Weight, bread ration, knife
and pencil from the list of names.**

24

Isolation camp of Kuç 1954-1958

The isolation camp of Kuç in Kurvelesh, Vlorö, 1957

Valentin Pervizi, Victor Dosti, Gulielm Deda and Thabit Rusi
Comaandaned years :   47   40   45

Ded
Gjoni, Thabit Rusi Prof .Dr. Mitat Aran
45　　　　　20　　　　　　45
4

Prof.Dr.Mitat Araniti (45)

Prof. Dr. Mitat Araniti (45)

Prof. Dr. Ali Cungu (20)

Prof. Dr. Alicungu (20)

Ylber Starova, Prof. Ali Cungu
(20)   (20)

Dr. Nedim Kokona (20)

Ingénieur Estref Frasheri, Dr. Latif Spahiu
(20)   (20)

Dr. Sander Saraçi,(20)

Dr. Loro Muzhani.(20)

Prof. Dr Ali Erebara. (20)

Prof. Guljelm Deda, (45)

Prof. Dr. Guljelm Deda (45)

Victor Dosti (40)

Victor Dosti (40)

Pjeter Bardheci, (15)

Fireplace in the painter's room

Dr. Ibrahim Sokoli (head) (20)

Dr. Ibrahim Sokoli, '20)

44

Back page, Fatbardh Kupi (45)

Tomorre Dine (45)

Tomorr Dine.(45)

Tomorr Dine (45)

Fatbarfh Kupi lisant un livre (45)

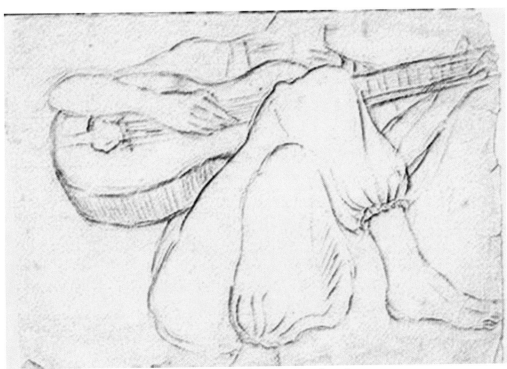

Cithariste de Kuç sans la tête,
Thabit Rusi (20)

Back page, young women, Kuç, 1957

Fight against a monster
Drawing for wooden sculpture

Fight against a monster
Realized in wood sculpture

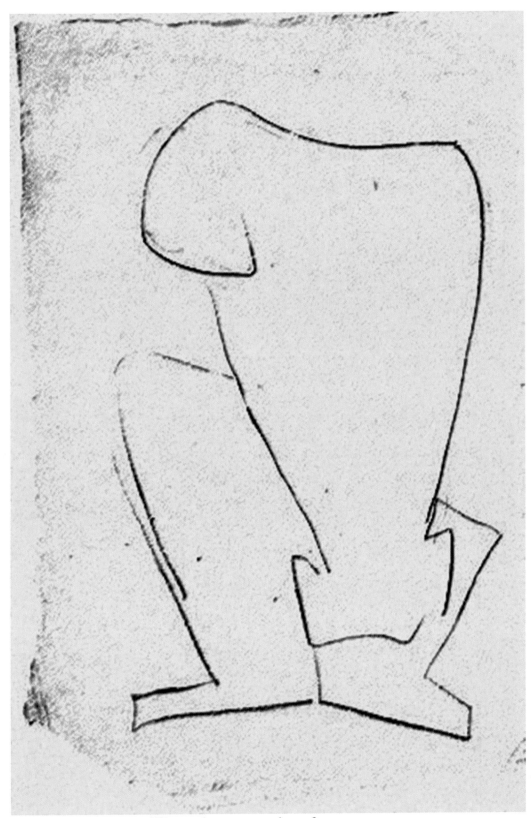

The prisoner project for monument

Gigantic plane trees of Kuç.

Project for the combat table of the Albanians against the Turks.

Gigantic plane of Kuç, natyral monument, 1957

Ruin of an old mill, kuç, 1957

Drawing of horses for battle of Scanderbeg; kuç, 1956

Pipe drawing with Prometheus figure failing sculpture, Kuç,1956

Drawing copied from Larousse loaned by Prof. Dr.. Ali Erebara, family friends.

Monalise de LeonardoDa Vinci drawn at the top of Kuç, 1957

Back page, diverf drawiwngs, Kuç, 1957

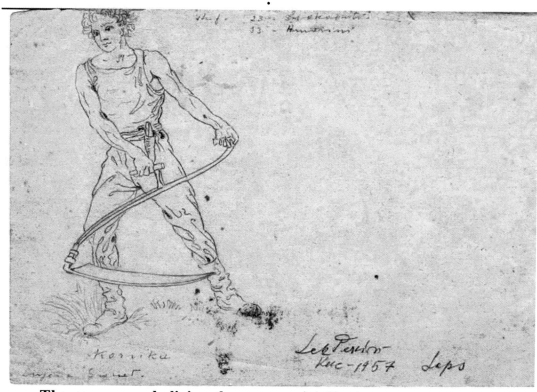

**The reaper symbolizing the communist dicature was strenuous
to mow innocent human life cobs, Kuç, 1957**

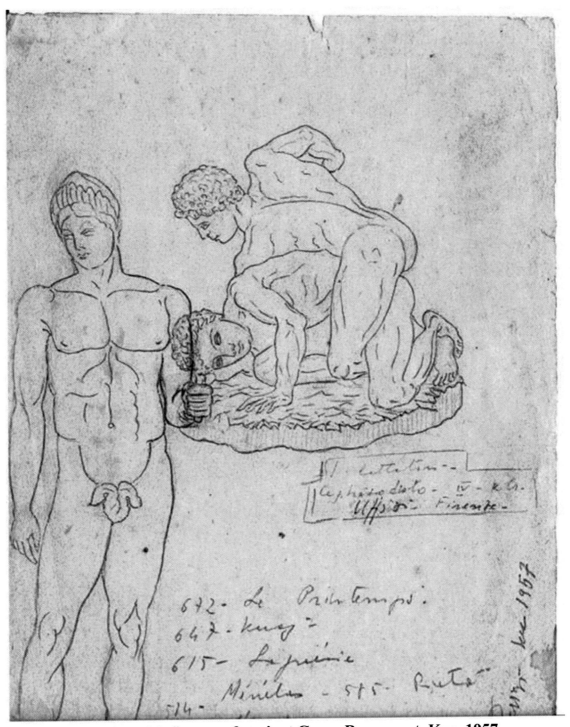

Exersice with figures of ancient Greco Roman art, Kuç, 1957.

Small mountain flowers among the rocks near the camp:Kuç,1956

Lule und
Sor Peruto Kue - 1156

61

Projekt per Vetro

Lek Pervizi
Kuç - 1957

Project for vases, Kuç, 1957

Women of Kuç for wooden sculpture, Kuç, 1957.

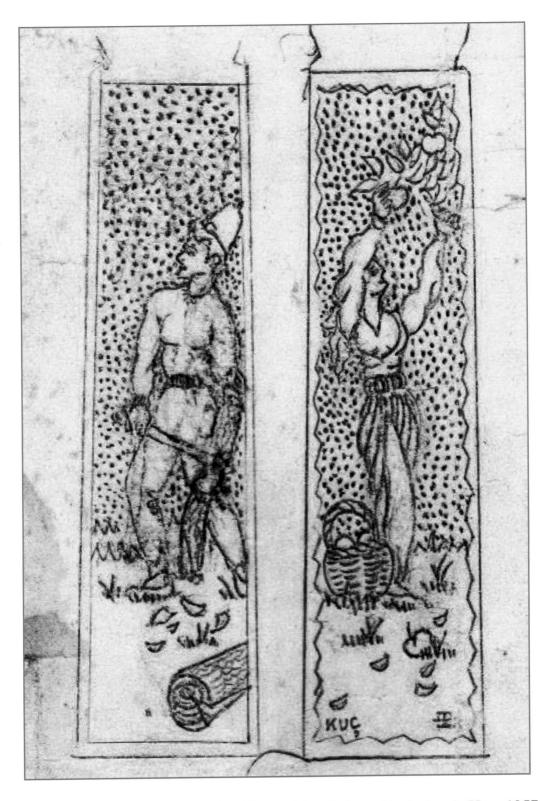

Drawing Wood table for neck gift t to friend, (pyroitechnique), Kuç, 1957

Young in traditional Kuç costumes, Kuç, 1957

Girls of kuç in tradfional costumes, Kuç, 1957

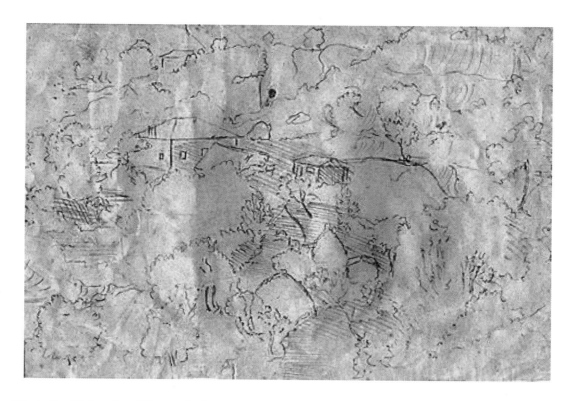

Huts built by families only in summer, came to see their dear ones, Kuç, 1956.

View of the mountain landscape from the camp position, Kuç, 1956

View of the mysterious mountain of ⬚ ika, Kuç 1957

Kuç, the mysterious mountain of ⬚ ika, covered with snow, Kuç 1957

Camp deof Pluk,Lushnjë
1958-1990

First period
Family patterns

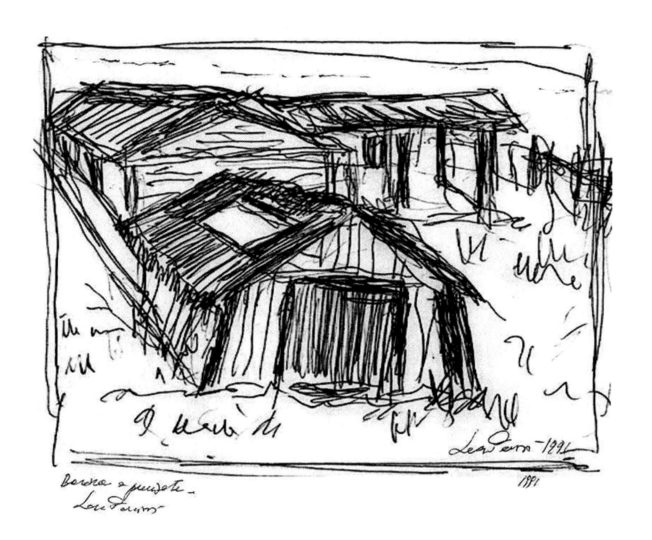

Barracks intended for the painter to work in conditions
unpleasant, with **Prof. Lazer Radi**, being designated
as enemies of the people and subject to the class struggle.

Selj-portrait, pluk, 1962

Self

Second brother Genz, Gradishtë, 1964
(40) and (42) years

Genz, 1967, Gradishtë, 4,

The brother of the painter Genz a
nd his two young daughter, Eva and Edi, Gradishtë 1974

Wife beba and chikdren, Pluk, 1968

Chidrensn Pluk, 1970

The little Aurel; Pluk, 1972

Drawing of Aurel, Pluk, 1974

Self-portrait profile and son, Pluk, 1978.

**Profile portrait of the painter's wife
Gjuliana or Beba. Pluk, 1968
42 years deported and displaced**

Portrait of Beba, knitting, Pluk, 1980.

Aurel, Pluk; 1984.

Aurel and the niece of the painter Eva,Pluk, 1983

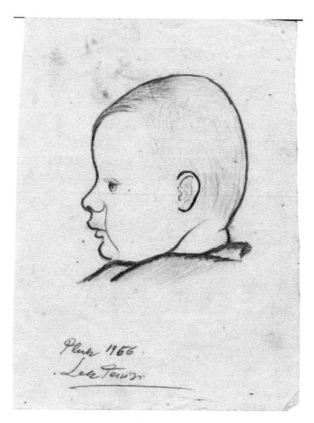

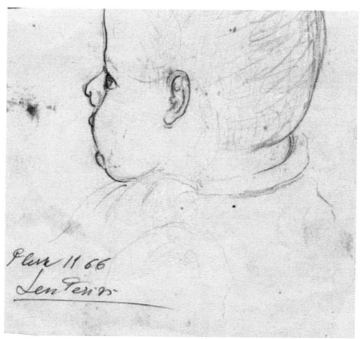

**Drawings of his first son, Leonarde,
t six months, Pluk, 1966**

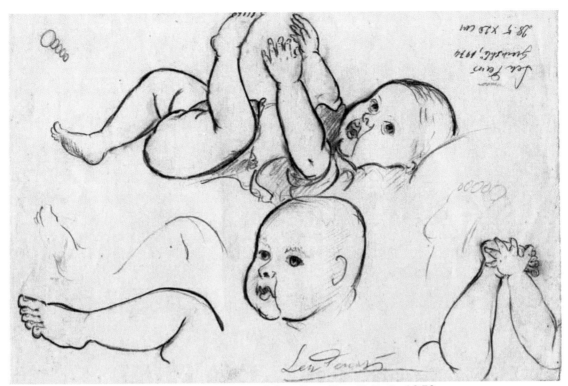

The firs chidren of family, Gradishtë, 1952

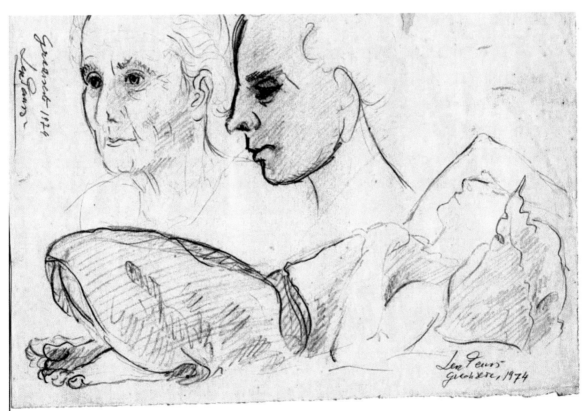

Back page, Mother, neighbor, and sleeping mother, 1967

Childrans, Pluk, 1966.

Back page, figures of men

Fieznd, Reshit Mulleti and Ernest Dosti, Lushnje, 1964
Deprtet 40 years.   rs

Deprted giirl in the Savre's camp, , Lusjnje, 1964

The swamp, site of the Gradishtë deportation camp, 1962

The great swamp of Karavasta, drawing for a hunting table.
place of depoertation., drawing, 1976
see below the back pag

**Back page, study design for stylized portrait
of his wife Beba, Pluk 1976**

Study for portrait of Beba,

Study for portrait of Beba

Study of stylized figure of Beba

Fiend Bajazit Kalosh, deprtated 45 years.,Pluk; 1976i

Study te tête de Scanderbeg, Pluk, 1982

Old house of Lushnjë, views from a balcony, and orthodox church, 1974

The painter's drawing s exhibited in the ruins of Tepelene camp

Shtëpia jonë e Laçit, djegur nga komunistët, shtator, 1944.

Veniice, pont et gondole, Pluk, 1980 (Chine ink

**Drawing by remembrance of the historic mountain houses of the Pervizi Skuraj,
Burnt down twice by the Turks (1878 and 1911) and the third by the
Communists, 1945.**

,

,

**End of all drawings of deportation camps of Tepelenë,
Kuç and Pluk of Lushnjë, 1951-1990, miraculously saved.**

Camp of Pluk of Luashnje
1965-1990
Second period

Old cattle stall, changed into a house, one room for family
including one to the painter. He had to add a swamp cane hut,
as a kitchen. In this house they lived there for 25 years, 1965-1990.

Under such painful conditions he had the courage and the strength to
demonstrate that he was a painter, condemned and forbidden to any free
expression.All these works remained unknown and hidden during the
period of the dictatorship. It is thanks to God, a real miracle, that they fled.

Self-portrait, special gravure on blass; Pluk;1976.

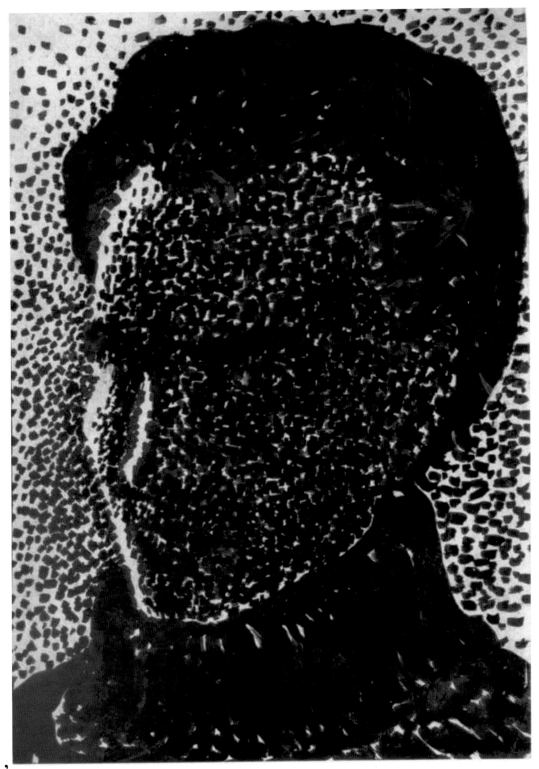

,

Self-portraits,chine ink , Pluk, 1978,

Self-portarit;, pencil on cardboard, Pluk, 1978

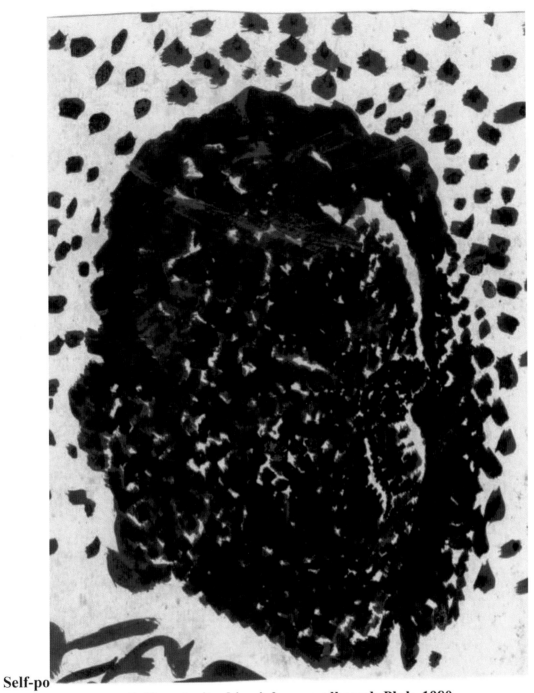

Self-po

Self-portarit, chine ink on cardboard; Pluk, 1980.

Drawings from the book of poems
"Great Lament"

These designs were possible in 1987, during the earthquake of communism which led to the fall of the dictatorship in Albania, to illustrate the poems conceived under the same conditions.

triwst sounds (self-portrait, Pluk, 1989.

Portopalermo, damned fortfres, Pluk, 1989

Holocaust of childrens, Pluk, 1989.

Great terror, Pluk, 1989

Mater Dolorosa, Pluk, 1989 (1).

Mater Dolorosa, Pluk, 1989 (2).

The weigh of the boot, Pluk, 1990

Monument au XX century. Pluk, 1980.

The bread's balade, Pluk. 1980

Behind the iron cage, Pluik, 1980

Immorttal Cross.

Sketch for a scene of terror

Caged

Drawing for a friend's prisoner grave

This is how I was reduced to a "living corpse"

The "tchianga", a metalic gong with a deafening soun

Plaques dedicated to the wife of painter, Beba, who escaped death of childrens in the camp of Tepelenë, witness to the crime against innocent victims, considered a heroine of deprtation camps.
The plaque's user, Grigor Kokali

Addition to the drawings

To this album we add three works by the same author, which are linked to the sequence of drawings by lek Pervizi. In fact, the first of three Great Lament books includes poems conceived exclusively in Tepelen's depressing field.

To Dante

Dante
sublime
and immortal poet
where were you?

In this earthly hell
you didn't appear
to describe
with your masterly verses
that abyss
demonic conception
of criminal mind

where the man
is changed
into skeletal osseous matter
and the bones
into powderinto nothing

the lament
of all a people
humiliated
for a piece of bread
thrown
like the bone to a dog

maybe you did not find
a glorious guide
a Virgil
and it is for this
that you would not undertake
the journey
between the depths of horror
where you must have heard
the desperate lamentation of mothers
for the trembling children
in the clutches of death

Dante
sublime
and immortal poet

Authouhouse publishing, 2020.

In the book Odyseey of Innocence, the incredible story is told of a man, 47 years old prisoner in prisons and deportation camps, and another 47 years separated from his Italian wife, co, whom he joins after half a century. The book is a journey between prisoners and deportation camps and is linked to the album drawings.

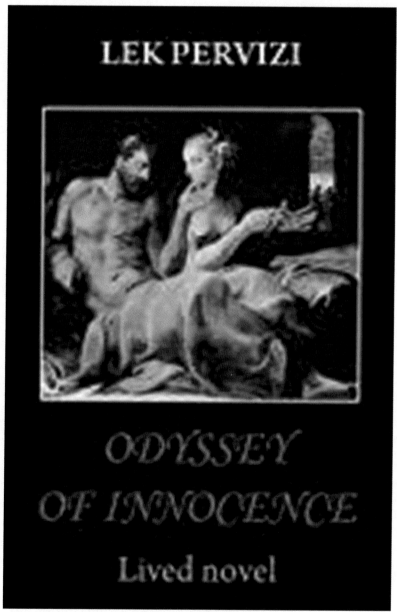

Authourhouse publishing, 2020

The third book; In the Circles of Hell forms a trilogy with the first two, because it tells of concrete facts captured from different people, political prisoners in prisons and camps of deprtation, subjected and tortured, and suffering throughout their half-century prison life.

Authourhouse publishing, 2021

Quotes from the books

The sun was rising over the mountains and day was dawning when the workers were leaving for another exhausting day of work. It was necessary to transport wood, beams, stones, fertilizer and other materials like beasts of burden, over tens of kilometers, from morning to late evening, without rest and without food, at the mercy of inclement weather and turmeil.

Albanian women and girls, old women and mothers with children, regardless of age and class, felt on their heads the weight of the hammer of dictatorship, which did not spare them to strike them with fury. Not only did they lose their lives under cruel torture, but those who were fortunate enough to live alive from that hell, lost their youth, were left cowards without families and children, dead alive.

There is no healthy and free human mind that can conceive of such monstrosities. But the communist dictatorship in Albania, led by a paranoid dictator with a criminal spirit like this Enver Hoxha, dealt with the creation of camps and prisons locked inside only innocent people, even the elderly, women and children. Is there a greater absurdity?

Conclusion:

These four works, contain in themselves the sad and tragic history of a people, never described in this way, in which the great bloody terror of the Communist dictatorship in Albania is highlighted, but which includes in itself the inhuman dictatorships of the twentieth century. These works that deserve to be awarded high prizes by the institutions humanitarian. It is quite clear that we are dealing with works of high documentary value and, as they determine with coincidental facts of how terrible and hateful the dictatorships were. In these works it is demonstrate that the infamous camp of deportation of Tepelena, is annovverato among the most terrible fields of steminnio of the dictatorships of the twentieth century. These works will certainly remain a reference to historians.

The Authour

It was at this age, 21, that Lek Pervizi was arrested and put in prison and concentration camps in 1950, where he spent 40 years of his life, an entire existence destroyed by the terror of the communist dictatorship of Albania, the harsher and fiercer among the other communist countries of eastern Europe.

Born in 1929, in a noble and promising Catholic family from the North of the country, he studied youth in Italy, Rome, where he spent 11 years of his life. This fact gives him the possibility of acquiring a strong culture, and of showing his talent as a poet and painter from an early age. This helps him to cope with the disastrous situation . In 1944 his family and him undergo the persecution of the communist regime. A persecution that begins with the burning of four field houses, preyand confiscated all to property. Deported grandmother, mother and her two brothers in prison. Cousins killed an died in prisons. His father, General Prenk Pervizi, a political refugee abroad, Greece, Italy and Belgium. Considered an enemy number one of the communist regime. It was the pretext for persecution, not for a few months or a few years, but covering the period 1944-1990. He had the chance to celebrate five years in Tirana, under the protection of a couple who had a bookstore, and held him as a comis. At that time he managed to enter the Lycée Artistic de Tirana with competition, where he claimed to be the best student, for his talent and also a promising young poet. But the Communists thought it other and he has just been arrested and put in prison and deported to the terrible depopulation camps of Portopalermo and of Tepelenë, where his nonagennial grandmother had already died, and locked up his mother, his brother and other relatives. . It was then that he found the courage to draw the place and the people locked in there monstrous barracks. The drawings and the poems remained unknown and hidden all the time of the dictatorship. It was after more than 50 years that the drawings came out, disturbing and shaking the minds of people, as well as of the governing authorities, that nothing was known about this camp, which is now in ruins and nothing else. Another aspect, the fact that there are no such drawings of Communist or Nazi concentration camps. A unique fact on a global scale. But having Albania as a small country and a small people, they did not pay attention due these drawings and poems. Conclusion; We had shown a photo when the painter was arrested in 1950 at the age of 21, and we show the photo of 2021, when he has joined the venerable age of 92 years old.

DANTE :
So, you are the painter
of these disturbing drawings?

AuthorHouse™ UK
1663 Liberty Drive
Bloomington, IN 47403 USA
www.authorhouse.co.uk
UK TFN: 0800 0148641 (Toll Free inside the UK)
UK Local: 02036 956322 (+44 20 3695 6322 from outside the UK)

Because of the dynamic nature of the Internet, any web addresses or links contained in this book may have changed
since publication and may no longer be valid. The views expressed in this work are solely those of the author and do
not necessarily reflect the views of the publisher, and the publisher hereby disclaims any responsibility for them.

Any people depicted in stock imagery provided by Getty Images are models,
and such images are being used for illustrative purposes only.
Certain stock imagery © Getty Images.

This book is printed on acid-free paper.

ISBN: 978-1-6655-8727-3 (sc)
ISBN: 978-1-6655-8728-0 (e)

Print information available on the last page.

Published by AuthorHouse 03/11/2021

authorHOUSE®

Printed in the United States
by Baker & Taylor Publisher Services